On the Front Line

FIGHTING THE VIETNAM WAR

Brian Fitzgerald

 Raintree

Chicago, Illinois

For information, address the publisher:
Raintree, 100 N. LaSalle, Suite 1200
Chicago, IL 60602
Customer Service: 888-363-4266
Visit our website at www.raintreelibrary.com

Printed and bound in China by South China Printing Company Ltd
09 08 07 06 05
10 9 8 7 6 5 4 3 2 1

Library of Congress Cataloging-in-Publication Data
Fitzgerald, Brian, 1972-
  Fighting the Vietnam War / Brian Fitzgerald.
     p. cm. -- (On the front line)
  Includes bibliographical references and index.
  ISBN 1-4109-1463-1 (library binding-hardcover) --
  ISBN 1-4109-1470-4 (pbk.)
1. Vietnamese Conflict, 1961-1975--Juvenile literature.
2. Vietnamese Conflict, 1961-1975--United States--Juvenile literature.
I. Title. II. Series.

DS557.7.F58 2005
959.704'3373--dc22

2005000290

Acknowledgments
The publishers would like to thank the following for permission to reproduce photographs and maps:
Art Archive pp. **17**, **27**; AKG p. **22**; Alamy p. **32**; Camerapress p. **9**; Corbis pp. **7**, **8**, **10**, **12**, **13**, **14**, **16**(l), **20**, **23**, **24**(l), **25**(r), **28**, **29**, **30**, **31**, **34–35**, **36**, **39**, **41**; Harcourt p. **26**; Popperfoto pp. **34**(l), **35**(r), **38**; Topfoto pp. **4–5**, **6**, **11**, **15**, **16**(r), **18**, **19**, **21**(l), **21**(r), **22**(l), **24–25**, **33**, **37**, **40**.

Cover photograph shows US troops loaded with equipment setting out on a patrol, reproduced with permission of AKG.

Map on p. 6 by Peter Bull.

Source notes: pp. **26–27** *The Tunnels of Cu Chi: The Untold Story of Vietnam* by Tom Mangold and John Penycate; pp. **28–29** Quote from Nguyen Cong Hoan taken from *Vietnam: A Portrait of its People at War* by David Chanoff and Doan Van Toai; pp. **34–35** Quote from Do Ba taken from a Thanh Nien newspaper article dated 16 March 1998; pp. **36–37** Quote from Nguyen Thi Duc taken from the documentary series *Vietnam: A Television History*; pp. **38–39** Quote from Colonel Bui Tin taken from the documentary series *Vietnam: A Television History*.

CONTENTS

Any words appearing in the text in bold, **like this,** are explained in the glossary. You can also look out for them in the Word Bank box at the bottom of each page.

A STRANGE NEW WORLD

International conflict

During the Vietnam War, the South Vietnamese fought against **Communist** troops from North Vietnam. The South Vietnamese were supported by troops from the United States, Australia, South Korea, New Zealand, the Philippines, and Thailand. Many questions about why the war was fought are still unanswered.

A U.S. Marine sergeant wades through a stream deep in the jungle of the Mekong Delta in Vietnam. He and the other ten members of his squad are exhausted. They have been on **patrol** for four days. Each man carries a heavy load of equipment through streams and jungles. The sound of machine gun fire is never far away. The sergeant knows he has to stay alert. Viet Cong **rebels** could surprise his squad at any moment. One false move might set off a **booby trap** that could kill him or one of his men. This is not the type of war he had expected. The battlefields are jungles and small villages.

American soldiers needed to stay alert during their patrols in Vietnam. Rivers and streams might contain hidden traps.

Word Bank   ally   country that is on the same side as another country during a war
patrol   search for enemy troops

The sergeant just needs to stay alive for two more months before his **tour of duty** will end and he can go home. His home seems like it is a million miles away. He is only twenty years old.

A new enemy

Only a few years earlier, most Americans could not find Vietnam on a map. During World War II the Vietnamese had helped the United States defeat Japan. Now the former **allies** were at war. Like so many others, including millions of people back home, the soldier wonders, "How did we get here?"

Find out later

What is Agent Orange?

What is a POW?

Who were the tunnel rats?

rebel person who fights against the people who are in power
tour of duty period of time spent in active military service

THE FIRST WAR

In the 1880s, France took control of the Asian countries of Vietnam, Laos, and Cambodia and named their new **colony** French Indochina. France grew rich from Vietnam's natural resources, but most Vietnamese people stayed poor. During World War II, the Japanese defeated the French in Vietnam. A **Communist** named Ho Chi Minh organized an army to free his homeland. Ho's army, called the Vietminh, used American weapons to fight the Japanese invaders. When Japan surrendered to the United States on September 2, 1945, Ho Chi Minh declared Vietnam a free nation.

Ho Chi Minh

Ho Chi Minh became a supporter of Communism while living in France. He brought his Communist beliefs back to his homeland and there he led the fight for Vietnam's independence until his death in 1969. His name means "he who **enlightens**."

A map of Vietnam showing the Ho Chi Minh Trail, and the sites of some of the key battles of the Vietnam War.

Ho Chi Minh Trail
Major battles
Borders
High ground
Low ground

NORTH VIETNAM
Dien Bien Phu
Hanoi
L
A
O
S
Gulf of Tonkin
Khe Sanh
Hamburger Hill
Hue
Da Nang
Ia Drang
CAMBODIA
SOUTH VIETNAM
Saigon
Mekong Delta

N
W   E
S

0   300 km
0   200 miles

Word Bank ambush surprise attack
artillery large mounted guns that fire shells or missiles

Fighting the French

A few weeks later, French troops returned to take back Vietnam. The Vietminh did not have the weapons to fight a normal battle. Instead they used **guerrilla** warfare. The Vietminh attacked French troops in hit-and-run **ambushes,** often at night. Over the next nine years, these tactics wore down the French troops' desire to fight.

In 1954, the French tried to force the Vietminh into a face-to-face battle in a valley in northern Vietnam called Dien Bien Phu. The Vietminh surprised the 16,500 French troops with an army of 50,000 soldiers. They pounded the French base with heavy **artillery** and quickly surrounded them. The French soldiers held out for 56 days before they finally surrendered on May 7, 1954. During the battle, 2,200 French soldiers and 8,000 Vietminh were killed.

Digging tunnels

An important weapon for the Vietminh at Dien Bien Phu was the shovel! They used shovels to dig tunnels and trenches that allowed them to surround the French troops and cut off their **supply lines.**

Vietnamese troops charge up a hill during the battle for Dien Bien Phu.

colony country or area that is ruled by another more powerful country
guerrilla soldier who is not part of a regular army

A divided country

The fighting between the Vietminh and the French occurred during the height of the **Cold War** between the **Soviet Union** and the United States. During their fight against the French, Ho Chi Minh's troops had received weapons and money from the Soviet Union and China. The United States did not want the **Communists** to gain power in Vietnam, so it spent more than a billion dollars to support the French.

After the defeat at Dien Bien Phu, France took its troops out of Vietnam. But Ho Chi Minh did not gain control of the whole country. A peace agreement split Vietnam into two parts. The Communists controlled North Vietnam.

Mini time line:

May 7, 1954—French surrender at Dien Bien Phu.

July 21, 1954—Vietnam is divided in half at a peace conference in Geneva, Switzerland.

March 1959—Ho Chi Minh declares a "people's war" to unite the divided country.

November 1960—John F. Kennedy elected U.S. president.

April 1961—Kennedy sends the first U.S. Special Forces to South Vietnam.

July 1962—Australia sends its first army advisers to South Vietnam.

An American military adviser trains South Vietnamese troops. →

Word Bank **Cold War** rivalry between the Soviet Union and the United States that began after World War II and lasted until the 1990s

The leaders of South Vietnam opposed Communism and gained the support of the United States. The land between the two areas was called the Demilitarized Zone, or DMZ.

The South under attack

Ho Chi Minh and the Communists wanted to control all of Vietnam. Communist **rebels** called the Viet Cong tried to gain power in the South. Most of the South Vietnamese army, called the Army of the Republic of Vietnam (ARVN), did not have the training or **combat** experience of the Viet Cong. The United States sent money, weapons, and military advisers to South Vietnam. However, U.S. President John F. Kennedy believed his country needed to do more. He increased the number of U.S. **Special Forces** soldiers in South Vietnam.

Ho Chi Minh Trail

The North Vietnamese moved weapons and supplies to the Viet Cong in South Vietnam along the Ho Chi Minh Trail (see page 6). Most people either walked or rode bicycles (see photo on the left). It could take as long as six months to move supplies down the Trail.

combat fighting
Special Forces top soldiers in the U.S. Army

THE UNITED STATES STEPS IN

Ap Bac

The battle of Ap Bac in South Vietnam was an early signal that the Viet Cong were a powerful enemy. On January 2, 1963, 350 Viet Cong soldiers defeated a South Vietnamese force that was four times larger and had better weapons.

United States **Special Forces** in South Vietnam were supposed to be there to teach the South Vietnamese army and native people how to use **guerrilla** warfare against the Viet Cong. But sometimes Special Forces troops found themselves in the middle of the fighting.

Battle at Nam Dang

On June 6, 1964, for example, the Viet Cong attacked a Special Forces camp at Nam Dong in South Vietnam. Captain Roger Donlon led the defense of the camp. He dodged heavy enemy gunfire and **grenades** as he rushed to close the main gate. There, he killed three Viet Cong soldiers who planned to blow up the gate. Donlon was shot in the stomach, but he kept fighting.

South Vietnamese soldiers guard two captured Viet Cong guerrillas while an American soldier looks on.

Word Bank ammunition bullets that are fired from a weapon
Medal of Honor top medal awarded by the U.S. Army

Donlon then ran to a **mortar** position where he found some of his men who had also been hit. He fired at the enemy and gave the injured men time to pull back. Donlon was hit by an enemy mortar round in the shoulder but he found the strength to move his mortar to a new position. There he found three more injured men.

Bravery awarded

Donlon was hit a third time as he dragged **ammunition** to his men, but still he did not stop fighting. Donlon's courage helped to inspire his men to victory. They finally defeated the Viet Cong at Nam Dong and Donlon became the first American soldier in Vietnam to earn a **Medal of Honor** from the U.S. Army. He is still alive today.

Agent Orange

In 1962, U.S. planes began spraying the chemical Agent Orange over South Vietnamese jungles, killing many thousands of trees (see photograph below). The United States hoped this would make it easier to spot the Viet Cong. Agent Orange was later found to cause cancer and birth defects.

mortar   small, portable cannon

New president, new strategy

On November 22, 1963, President Kennedy was **assassinated.** Lyndon Johnson took over as president of the United States. Johnson was worried about Vietnam. The Viet Cong were growing stronger in South Vietnam. Johnson wanted to send more troops, but he knew most Americans would not support that.

Attack in the Gulf of Tonkin

On August 2, 1964, the USS *Maddox* was sailing off the Vietnamese coast in the Gulf of Tonkin. Three North Vietnamese **patrol** boats appeared and began heading toward the **destroyer.** The commander of the *Maddox*, Herbert L. Ogier, ordered his crew to fire three warning shots. When the patrol boats ignored the warning, the *Maddox* opened fire.

Bombing targets

U.S. President Johnson wanted to end the war quickly without losing too many American soldiers. He sent U.S. warplanes to bomb the Ho Chi Minh Trail and other key targets in North Vietnam. This operation was called Rolling Thunder.

President Johnson (second from right) met with his advisers on August 4, 1964 to discuss the crisis in the Gulf of Tonkin.

Word Bank   assassinated murdered
destroyer fast, lightly armored but heavily armed warship

The *Maddox* scored one direct hit and damaged a second boat. The *Maddox* also avoided two **torpedoes** launched by one of the boats. Two days after leaving the Gulf, the *Maddox* and another destroyer named *Turner Joy* returned. The crews of both ships reported being attacked. The United States then sent F-8 jet planes to attack North Vietnamese patrol boats in the area.

The President gains power

President Johnson believed the attacks showed that the North Vietnamese wanted to start a war with the United States and much of the American public now agreed with him. He asked the U.S. Congress to approve the Gulf of Tonkin **Resolution.** This gave the President the power to use any means he needed to stop further attacks.

What happened?

There is no real proof that the second attack, involving the *Maddox* and *Turner Joy* (see photograph below), really happened. The North Vietnamese deny firing at the U.S. ships. American crews claimed that they hit at least three enemy boats, but no wreckage or bodies were ever found.

resolution formal decision that is agreed upon by a vote
torpedo missile that is fired underwater

DANGER IN THE AIR

Thunder rolls on

Operation Rolling Thunder was supposed to last a few months, but it went on for more than three years. Thousands of Vietnamese were killed. Many bridges, roads, and buildings were hit, but were soon repaired. The Ho Chi Minh Trail also stayed open. The **campaign** had failed.

Captain Merlyn Dethlefsen climbed into his F-105 Thunderchief plane. He was about to take off on a Rolling Thunder bombing mission deep in North Vietnam. His target was a **surface-to-air missile (SAM)** site that protected an important steel factory. His mission was to destroy the SAMs so other American bombers could destroy the steelworks without being fired at.

Things did not go as planned, however. The SAM site was surrounded by **artillery.** The sky was filled with black clouds from enemy gunfire. Dethlefsen flew toward the ground to avoid missiles from attacking **MiG** jet fighters. His plane was badly damaged by a shell from an enemy cannon.

00315

Word Bank   campaign   series of related missions that form a phase of a war

Mission complete

Dethlefsen could have headed for safety, but he knew the bombers would not stand a chance against the SAMs. The lives of the American crews depended on him. Dethlefsen made five passes over the steelworks. He dodged fire from 96 enemy cannons on the ground and four **MiG** fighters in the air. The brave captain destroyed two SAM sites.

Just doing his job

Dethlefsen's bravery allowed the bomber pilots to wipe out their targets without losing any planes. "All I did was the job I was sent to do," Dethlefsen later said. He had bravely completed his mission and safely made it back to his base. Many other American pilots would not be so lucky.

Napalm

U.S. planes did not just drop bombs. Many also dropped **napalm.** This sticky gel made from gasoline burst into flames when it hit the air. Napalm was meant to destroy military targets, but it also burned thousands of **civilians**. The child in the photograph above was badly burned in a napalm strike.

A flight of three F-105s refuel in the air on their way to bombing targets in North Vietnam in 1966.

civilian   person who is not in the armed forces

Shot down over Hanoi

In October 1967, U.S. Navy pilot John McCain took off on a bombing raid. His target was Hanoi, the capital of North Vietnam. He did not return for more than five years. An enemy missile blew off his plane's right wing. McCain ejected from his plane. The force broke his right knee and both his arms.

McCain landed in a lake and almost drowned. An angry mob pulled him to shore. Troops soon arrived to take him away. McCain was taken to a prison that American pilots called the Hanoi Hilton. He became a **prisoner of war (POW)**.

These captured U.S. pilots were forced to march through the streets of Hanoi.

John McCain (bottom right) poses with other U.S. Navy pilots in 1965. He later became a U.S. senator.

Word Bank   missing in action   term used to describe a soldier who does not return from a war alive and whose body is never found

Prisoner of war

McCain lay in an empty cell for four days before his captors took him to hospital. A doctor put one of McCain's arms in a cast. He did not fix the other arm. McCain did not receive an operation on his knee for more than a month.

The North Vietnamese tried to force him to tell them military secrets. McCain refused. The guards put him in his own cell. He was not allowed to see or talk to other prisoners for two years. Later, they planned to release McCain, but he refused to leave his fellow prisoners behind. The guards made him pay by **torturing** him for four days. He was not released until March 1973.

POWs and MIAs

- 802 prisoners were released by North Vietnam at the end of the war.

- 661 of these were U.S. military men. Nearly 500 were pilots who had been shot down.

- 141 were **civilians**.

- 36 prisoners escaped during the war.

- 2,583 U.S. military personnel were listed as **missing in action (MIA)**.

This North Vietnamese poster calls the United States a "paper tiger." This meant that it was not as powerful as it seemed. The **Communists** used anti-United States posters like this one to try to win new supporters in South Vietnam.

torture beatings and pain inflicted on prisoners, often to get secret information out of them

On March 8, 1965, the first U.S. ground troops arrived in Vietnam. Their job was to protect the base at Da Nang, so planes could safely carry out bombing missions in North Vietnam.

The draft

The United States' new plan in Vietnam needed many more troops. The U.S. government began to **draft** young men between the ages of 18 and 25 for military service. More than two million American men were drafted between 1965 and 1972.

The search begins

The original mission of the U.S. troops had been to defend key positions in the south. However, soldiers from the North Vietnamese army now supported the Viet Cong. The South Vietnamese army alone could not stop its enemies from gaining control of the towns and villages in South Vietnam. The United States decided to adopt a new strategy called "search and destroy." U.S. troops would hunt down their enemy and wipe it out. By the end of the year, more than 180,000 U.S. troops had arrived in Vietnam.

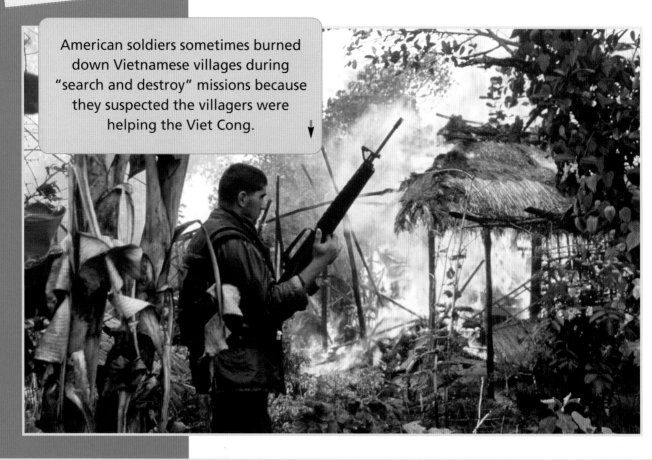

American soldiers sometimes burned down Vietnamese villages during "search and destroy" missions because they suspected the villagers were helping the Viet Cong.

Word Bank   covert   secret
draft   order someone into military service

Early clashes

U.S. troops faced the North Vietnamese army for the first time in the Battle of Ia Drang, which was at its fiercest from November 14–17, 1965. The North Vietnamese army had more men, but the U.S. troops had air support from **gunships** and bombers. The North Vietnamese army suffered more than 2,500 casualties and was pushed out of the area.

The North Vietnamese lost the battle, but they learned an important lesson. They did not have the firepower to match the United States. For the rest of the war they would use the same **guerrilla** tactics that had helped them defeat the French. They would try to break the Americans' will to keep fighting.

Help from "down under"

The United States was not the only country to send troops to support South Vietnam. South Korea sent more than 300,000 troops and Australia sent about 50,000 soldiers. Members of the Australian Special Air Service sometimes teamed up with U.S. Green Berets for **covert** missions.

An Australian soldier wearing a jungle "boonie" hat takes cover behind a tree.

gunship   helicopter that is armed with several guns or rockets

Help from above

Helicopters played a huge role in Vietnam. Soldiers called them "Hueys" or choppers. Choppers were used to transport troops in and out of **hostile** territory. They often needed to fly very close to enemy fire. The men who flew choppers were extremely brave.

On November 14, during the Battle of Ia Drang, a **battalion** of American soldiers was surrounded by North Vietnamese troops. The Americans were running low on **ammunition.** Their commander would not let any helicopters land because it was too dangerous. One pilot knew the men needed help, so he decided to land anyway.

U.S. troops jump from a Huey into battle. The helicopter played an important role in the Vietnam War.

Word Bank   battalion   large military unit made up of 300 to 1,000 troops

A heroic pilot

Captain Ed Freeman flew through heavy gunfire to deliver ammunition, water, and medical supplies to the soldiers on the ground. He made the trip many times, even though his helicopter was not armed with any weapons. Without his bravery, many more troops might have been killed.

Many of the soldiers on the ground were injured. Medical choppers refused to fly into the area. They did not want to risk getting shot down. Freeman knew the men might die without medical care. He and his crew flew fourteen separate missions to **evacuate** the injured. They rescued more than 30 wounded men. Freeman lived to tell his incredible story of bravery. He retired from the U.S. Army in 1967.

Mail call

Choppers brought many supplies to soldiers. Some soldiers say the most important delivery was the mail. Soldiers in Vietnam had no other contact with family or friends. A letter from home could help them forget about the horrors of war.

An injured U.S. Marine is carried to a helicopter.

evacuate move to safety
hostile unfriendly

21

Trouble in the jungle

The search and destroy missions led U.S. troops into the jungles of Vietnam. Small squads of about a dozen men moved through the mud and **rice paddies.** These foot soldiers were nicknamed "grunts."

Each man carried all his equipment on his back. These packs could weigh as much as 70 pounds (32 kilograms). Soldiers and their equipment often got tangled in vines. They called these "wait a minute vines" because one grunt had to tell the rest of his squad to "wait a minute" while he tried to remove the vines. Vietnam has a tropical **climate.** This meant that grunts in the jungle were usually wet and cold during the **monsoon season** and hot and sweaty in the summer.

Booby traps

Grunts needed to watch out for booby traps such as:

- Toe popper—a bullet placed on a sharp bamboo stake that would fire when stepped on.
- Punji stakes—sharp bamboo stakes placed in a small hole and covered with leaves (see photograph below).

U.S. troops loaded with gear set out on a patrol.

Word Bank climate weather conditions for a certain area
monsoon season period of wind and rain in southern Asia

Grunts also had to be careful not to set off **booby traps.** **Tripwires** tied between trees on land or in streams could set off hidden bombs.

Invisible enemy

The Viet Cong liked to hide in the thick jungle. They **ambushed** U.S. troops without any warning. Grunts did not get much sleep because they knew the Viet Cong often attacked at night. Soldiers grew frustrated because they often could not see their enemy. There was no way to tell an innocent farmer from an enemy soldier. The frequent **guerrilla** attacks by the Viet Cong took many lives and also damaged **morale.**

A grunt takes a break from patrol to eat his C-rations.

Chow time

Soldiers on **patrol** usually ate **combat rations** (C-rations). A C-ration box might contain a can of hot dogs and beans, peaches, and a piece of cake. The box would also include salt, pepper, sugar, chewing gum, toilet paper, and cigarettes.

tripwire wire stretched close to the ground that sets off an explosion when touched

R and R

Soldiers who returned from patrols were sometimes given a few days of rest and relaxation (called "R and R"). Many soldiers went to Saigon, the South Vietnamese capital. Others went to camps that had beautiful beaches where they could swim and sunbathe, as shown in the photograph below.

Trouble in the water

Small U.S. Navy boats called swift boats **patrolled** the Mekong Delta in South Vietnam. The Americans did not want the Viet Cong to use the river as a **supply line.** They also wanted to capture or kill the many Viet Cong soldiers who hid along the waterway.

John Kerry was in charge of a swift boat and its five-man crew. One night, on March 19, 1969, Kerry was told that another boat had come under attack. Kerry and his crew rushed to help. A Viet Cong rocket exploded near his boat. Kerry ordered his crew to beach the boat on the shore. He jumped off the boat.

Word Bank   detonated   exploded

On the beach, Kerry saw a Viet Cong soldier with a rocket launcher. One rocket could destroy the boat and kill his crew. Kerry killed the Viet Cong soldier before he could fire at the boat.

Swift action

On March 28, 1969, Kerry's boat came under fire again. A mine blew up near his boat. Kerry's arm was injured when a second mine **detonated**. Kerry discovered that one of his men had fallen overboard. Enemy **snipers** were firing at the man in the water. Kerry knew he had to save his fellow soldier. He ordered his crew to fire at the enemy. Kerry's arm was bleeding and he was in pain, but he still reached into the water and pulled the man on to his boat.

Purple Hearts

John Kerry received three Purple Heart medals for his actions in Vietnam. When he returned to the United States he became a vocal **protester** against the war and later became a U.S. senator. In 2004 he ran for president of the United States, but was beaten by George W. Bush.

Three U.S. patrol boats cruise the Mekong River in search of Viet Cong **guerrillas.**

MEET THE PRESS

JOHN KERRY "Vietnam Veterans Against the War"

In April 1971, John Kerry (right) appeared on a popular American television news program called *Meet the Press* to speak out against the Vietnam War.

sniper hidden soldier who shoots enemy soldiers from long distances with a special gun

25

The underground world

The Viet Cong also faced many dangers. They built a series of tunnels in South Vietnam to hide from U.S. troops and take cover from bombs. They did not have many resources so they had to come up with some very clever ways to survive.

Hospital under fire

Viet Cong doctor Vo Hoang Le had been operating on patients for three days. Le did not work in an ordinary hospital. It was located 15 feet (5 meters) underground! Some of the instruments he used were made from parts of shot-down American planes and helicopters.

American troops were moving toward the tunnel that led to the hospital. Le's medical staff wanted to retreat.

The Viet Cong used underground cities such as this one to hide from U.S. attacks.

tripwire mine

smoke outlets

kitchen

meeting place

concrete trap doors

hand-detonated mines

false tunnel with booby trap grenade

booby trap

ventilation shaft to let air in

to rest of tunnel system

sleeping area

place for wounded to be treated

well

storage area for food, weapons, and explosives

water-filled U-bend prevents gas from passing into rest of tunnel

tunnel hospital for seriously wounded

Word Bank   spider hole   small one-person hole that is covered with leaves

However, Le could not let his 60 wounded patients be captured. He hid in a **spider hole** and waited. Eventually, Le saw three American soldiers moving toward him. Very frightened, but determined, he fired his gun. All three soldiers fell to the ground. The doctor had become a soldier.

Amazing courage

A few months later, Le was defending another hospital when he was shot in the right hand. He was bleeding badly and his little finger was hanging by a piece of skin. Le tore his finger off and bandaged his hand. He could no longer use his right hand, so he taught himself how to perform **surgery** left-handed.

Oh rats!

The brave U.S. soldiers who explored Viet Cong tunnels were known as tunnel rats. They carried a pistol, a knife, and a torch into the dark, narrow tunnels. There they faced many dangers including **booby traps**, snakes, and being shot by Viet Cong soldiers.

This soldier is being lowered into a tunnel as part of a search and destroy mission.

surgery medical operation

THE TIDE TURNS

Surprise attack

The Tet Offensive also surprised South Vietnamese **civilians.** Nguyen Cong Hoan remembers the terror of the surprise attack:

"It began around midnight with what everyone first thought were firecrackers. When we realized a battle was going on we rushed out of the house and ran toward the beach. Thousands of people were on the beach watching the explosions and the planes swooping down and the great balls of orange fire."

In January 1968, both sides agreed to stop fighting so that Vietnamese soldiers on both sides could celebrate their new year, called "Tet." Many South Vietnamese troops went home to their families. On January 30, Viet Cong and North Vietnamese troops broke the **truce.** More than 80,000 troops launched a surprise assault on more than 100 South Vietnamese cities in the attack known as the Tet Offensive.

The Tet Offensive

Many of the troops focused on taking key buildings in Saigon, the capital of South Vietnam. Viet Cong **guerrillas** broke into the grounds of the U.S. **embassy** and killed four Americans. The embassy was not made safe until several hours later. Despite the initial losses, however, the U.S. military quickly recovered from the surprise attack. They took back most of the country in only a few days.

U.S. troops attempt to secure the streets of Saigon after the Tet Offensive of 1968.

Word Bank   embassy   government building of one country that is located in a foreign country

In the ancient city of Hue, a bloody battle raged for nearly a month. U.S. troops fought through the streets to regain control of the city. The **Communists** were finally driven out. Most of Hue's buildings had been destroyed during the battle. More than 100,000 people became **refugees.**

A losing victory?

The Communists had hoped their attack would cause the South Vietnamese people to rise up against their government. They did not achieve their goal. The Communists lost ten times as many men as the United States and the South Vietnamese army. The Tet Offensive was a military victory for the United States, but it was a major defeat in other ways.

A long siege

About a week before Tet, the North Vietnamese attacked a U.S. Marine base at Khe Sanh. It was not a very important base, but the United States refused to let it fall. The siege of Khe Sanh lasted 77 days before North Vietnamese forces were driven out.

U.S. Marines fire a heavy machine gun at North Vietnamese troops during the battle of Khe Sanh. ↓

refugee   person forced to leave home, usually during a war
truce   agreement to stop fighting

Trouble at home

At the beginning of 1968, many Americans believed the United States was close to winning the war. Since the fighting had started, U.S. troops had not lost any major battles. After the Tet Offensive many people changed their minds. It seemed now that the **Communists** were still very powerful and that the United States could not win the war.

Protests

Major war **protests** had been taking place in the United States since 1965. Many Americans did not think their country should be fighting an enemy that was not a direct threat to the United States. As the war dragged on, Americans grew tired of sending their young men to die in Vietnam.

Images like this one of three wounded American soldiers were very common during the Vietnam War. They started to turn Americans against the war.

Word Bank demonstration group protest
draft card official letter ordering a person to enter the military

The protests increased after the Tet Offensive. People from all walks of life joined **demonstrations** calling for an end to the war. Students on college campuses refused to go to lectures. Many young men burned their **draft cards.** Others went to Canada or Europe to avoid going to war. Even many **veterans** of the war joined in the protest movement.

New leader

In March 1968, President Johnson announced that he would not run for reelection. He was worn down by the war in Vietnam and the protests at home. Another president would have to find a way to end the war. In November 1968, Richard Nixon was elected U.S. president.

Racism?

Many college students were excused from the **draft** until they finished college. But people with low incomes, many of whom were black, could not usually afford college. Many African Americans believed the draft was **racist** because it singled out people with less education, many of whom were black.

War protesters block the entrance to the U.S. Capitol building in Washington DC.

---

racist someone who hates someone else because of the color of their skin
veteran person who served in the armed forces

A PROMISE OF PEACE

Before the election, President Nixon had promised to bring "peace with honor." He said he had a plan for ending the war, not winning it. He called it "Vietnamization." This meant that the South Vietnamese army would take over most of the fighting, using American weapons and being trained by U.S. troops. Then the Americans would be able to go home.

Nixon's plan

Many things went wrong with the plan. The South Vietnamese army was in bad shape. Many officers were not good leaders. Soldiers did not have enough time to train and seemed afraid to fight. They were used to having U.S. troops fight for them. Many South Vietnamese troops deserted.

Army drug abuse

Many troops used drugs in Vietnam. Studies showed that more than half of U.S. troops smoked cannabis. Some others used more dangerous drugs, like **heroin**. Drugs ruined the lives of many soldiers who became **addicts**.

Many American soldiers wanted peace in Vietnam just as much as the people back in the United States.

Word Bank   addict   person who cannot stop doing something or using something
deserted   left without permission

Soldiers want out

Nixon's plan hurt the **morale** of the U.S. troops. Their goal had been to win the war. Now, they just wanted to get home alive. No one wanted to be the last soldier to die in Vietnam. They knew about the war **protests** back in the United States. Many soldiers were also against the war. Some refused to follow orders to fight. Others deserted their **platoons.**

Officers as targets

Many soldiers disliked their commanding officers. Some thought officers cared more about their own careers than the lives of their men. These troops "fragged" their commanders. This meant they tried to kill or injure the officers by throwing **grenades** or shooting at them. Nearly 800 cases of fragging were reported in Vietnam.

Battle for Hamburger Hill

The battle for Hamburger Hill, in May 1969, showed why many people were against the war. Seventy U.S. soldiers died and 372 were wounded. But the army abandoned the hill shortly after taking it because they thought that they did not need it to win the battle. All the bloodshed had been for no good reason.

U.S. troops rush a wounded soldier to a helicopter during the battle for Hamburger Hill.

heroin harmful, illegal drug
platoon small army unit usually made up of 16 to 44 men

Frightened children

Do Ba was only eight years old at the time of the My Lai massacre. Here, he remembers the horrors of having to hide under dead bodies:

"I was small so I was buried among the dead bodies of others. My whole body was soaked with their blood."

Vietnamese civilians often found themselves in the line of fire. Here, an elderly woman and her grandchild take cover in a field.

More problems for Nixon

President Nixon had other problems to face back in the United States. In November 1969, the public learned of the horrible **massacre** of hundreds of Vietnamese **civilians.**

Revenge mission

More than a year earlier, a **platoon** of American soldiers had arrived in a small village called My Lai. The men had been told that many Viet Cong troops were in the area. The U.S. troops wanted revenge for their friends who had been killed or injured by **booby traps** and **snipers.**

Word Bank　　horrified shocked
　　　　　　　　massacre killing of a large number of innocent people

The U.S. troops found only women, children, and old men in the village. Not a single shot was fired at the American soldiers. But they still wanted revenge. They took out their anger on the helpless villagers. Over the next four hours, the U.S. troops murdered as many as 500 innocent people. The troops slaughtered the very people they were supposed to be protecting.

Outrage

The My Lai massacre was kept secret for more than a year. Once the truth came out, Americans were **outraged** that their government had lied to them. They were even angrier that a small group of U.S. troops could commit such an awful crime. Even Americans who supported the war were **horrified**.

Student deaths

On May 4, 1970, U.S. National Guard troops were called in to break up a war **protest** at Kent State University in Ohio. The soldiers shot **tear gas** into the crowd of students, but the protesters still did not leave (see photograph below). The troops then started shooting at unarmed students. Four died and nine others were injured. The violence shocked the world and sparked hundreds more protests around the United States.

This elderly South Vietnamese man is being led away by a U.S. soldier who suspects him of supporting the Viet Cong.

outraged made very angry
tear gas type of gas that makes your eyes fill with tears

THE UNITED STATES PULLS OUT

Peace talks between the United States and the **Communists** from North Vietnam had begun in 1968. The talks dragged on for several years. Both sides wanted to end the war, but neither wanted to give up too much to its enemy. In October 1972, they finally agreed on a settlement.

No deal

The South Vietnamese did not like the terms of the settlement. They also knew their country would collapse without the help of the Americans so they refused to sign the deal. This angered the North Vietnamese. The peace talks ground to a halt. On December 18, 1972, President Nixon ordered a massive bombing raid on Hanoi. This became known as the Christmas bombings.

The Christmas bombings left much of Hanoi in ruins.

Word Bank   cease-fire end to fighting

36

The Christmas bombings

Over twelve days, giant B-52 bombers dropped thousands of tons of bombs on Hanoi. It was the most intense bombing attack of the war. The North Vietnamese finally agreed to negotiate again. They did not want to see any more of their homeland destroyed.

A new agreement

The United States and North Vietnam reached a new deal. The South Vietnamese had no choice but to approve it. The last U.S. **combat** troops left Vietnam on March 29, 1973. More than 58,000 Americans had been killed. More than 300,000 were wounded. Billions of dollars had been spent and nothing had been gained. The South Vietnamese were now left to fight alone.

A former U.S. prisoner of war is reunited with his family in March 1973.

Peace details

The 1973 peace agreement stated that:

- there would be a **cease-fire** in Vietnam.

- armies on both sides would keep whatever land they currently held.

- U.S. troops would leave Vietnam within 60 days.

- all **prisoners of war** would be returned.

Renewed fighting

Both the North and South Vietnamese soon broke the peace agreement. The two sides once again fought to control the land in South Vietnam. The South Vietnamese were no longer protected by the experienced U.S. troops. The South Vietnamese army was running out of supplies and **morale** was low.

The United States had promised to help South Vietnam if the **Communists** broke the peace agreement. But when the fighting broke out, the United States did not respond. American leaders were no longer interested in supporting this unpopular war.

One last assault

In early 1975, the North Vietnamese made a final attack. They quickly swept through many South Vietnamese cities. South Vietnam's president ordered his troops to retreat.

He needed them to defend the capital of Saigon. Thousands of troops **deserted** instead. More than 500,000 **refugees** moved into Saigon. By the middle of April the North Vietnamese army had surrounded the city.

Saigon falls

On April 30, 1975, North Vietnamese army tanks and trucks rolled into the South Vietnamese capital. The streets were filled with weapons and uniforms left behind by South Vietnamese army troops. Tanks burst through the gates of the presidential palace. The South Vietnamese president quickly surrendered. The Communists renamed the capital Ho Chi Minh City after their heroic leader. After 30 years, the war was over.

North Vietnamese troops show their flag after capturing the presidential palace in Saigon.

Entering Saigon

The North Vietnamese met little resistance in the South Vietnamese capital. Colonel Bui Tin remembers:

"That night [April 30], when I sprawled on the lawn of the Independence Palace with members of a communication unit, we all agreed it was the happiest day of our lives because it was a day of complete victory for the nation, because the war ended."

After the war

In October 1978 Chau Van Nguyen, his wife, and three young children boarded a small boat in Saigon. The boat was crowded with people all trying to escape from Vietnam. The Nguyens' boat almost turned over during a terrible **hurricane.** A tanker from Taiwan saved them. The family stayed on the boat for twenty days. They were packed into a tight space and did not have much food.

Chau's family was taken to Taiwan. They lived in a camp with other Vietnamese **refugees.** More than a year later, an American church paid for the Nguyen family to live in New York state. Many American churches helped Vietnamese refugees with clothes, food, and shelter.

Boat people

The war left much of Vietnam in ruins. As many as three million Vietnamese people may have died. Thousands were left without homes or jobs. People fled from Vietnam on boats, searching for a better life (see photograph below, taken in Saigon in the final days of the war). More than one million Vietnamese people settled in the United States alone.

Word Bank   hurricane   severe storm with heavy winds and rain

The United States' pain

People in the United States also suffered after the war. The United States had never lost a war until Vietnam. It was the longest and most costly war the United States had ever fought. Many Americans wanted to forget about Vietnam. To some, this meant forgetting about the men who had fought so bravely. Vietnam **veterans** were not treated as heroes like the soldiers of past wars. Many found it difficult to return to normal life. They could not forget the horror of war. In the years since the war ended, the wounds of the veterans and the nation slowly began to heal. Only in 2000 did the United States finally start trading with Vietnam again.

Fitting tribute

In 1982 the Vietnam Veterans' Memorial opened in Washington D.C. The long granite wall lists the names of more than 58,000 U.S. soldiers who died or are still missing in Vietnam. The memorial honors all the American men and women who bravely served during the conflict. It aims to ensure that the soldiers who died in Vietnam will never be forgotten.

TIME LINE

1945
September 2   Ho Chi Minh declares Vietnam's independence from France.

1946
December   French troops force the Vietminh out of Hanoi.

1954
May 7   French surrender at Dien Bien Phu.
July 21   Vietnam is officially divided into North Vietnam and South Vietnam.

1960
November 8   John F. Kennedy is elected U.S. president.

1963
January 2   Viet Cong troops defeat the South Vietnamese army at Ap Bac.
November 22   President Kennedy is **assassinated** and Lyndon Johnson takes over as president.

1964
August 2   U.S. destroyer USS *Maddox* is attacked by three North Vietnamese **patrol** boats in the Gulf of Tonkin.

1965
March 2   Rolling Thunder bombing **campaign** begins.
March 8   The first U.S. **combat** troops arrive at Da Nang, South Vietnam.
October–
November   The Battle of Ia Drang is fought.

1968
January 21   The siege of Khe Sanh begins.
January 30   The Tet Offensive begins.
February 24   The bloody battle for Hue ends.
March 16   My Lai **massacre**.

March 31	President Johnson announces he will not run for reelection.
November 5	Richard Nixon is elected president of the United States.

1969

April 30	Number of U.S. troops in Vietnam reaches 543,400.
May 20	The ten-day battle for Hamburger Hill ends.
June 8	Nixon announces the first withdrawals of U.S. troops from Vietnam.
September 2	Ho Chi Minh dies in Hanoi.
November 15	More than 250,000 people take part in a war **protest** in Washington D.C. It is the largest war protest in American history.

1970

May 4	Four students protesting against the war at Kent State University, Ohio, are killed by National Guard troops.

1971

August 18	Australia announces that most of its troops will leave South Vietnam by the end of the year.

1972

December 18	Christmas bombings of Hanoi and Haiphong by the United States begin.

1973

January 27	Peace agreement is signed in Paris, France.
February 12	The first group of U.S. **prisoners of war** is released from North Vietnamese prison camps.
March 29	The last U.S. combat troops leave Vietnam.

1975

April 30	North Vietnamese troops take Saigon.

FIND OUT MORE

Books

Here are just a few of the many books about the Vietnam War.

Burgan, Michael. *Witness to History: The Vietnam War*. Chicago: Heinemann, 2005.

Dunn, John M. *American War Library: The Vietnam War: A History of U.S. Involvement*. Farmington Hills, Mich.: Lucent Books, 2001.

Ferguson, Amanda. *American Women of the Vietnam War*. New York: Rosen Publishing Group, 2004.

Gavin, Philip. *The Fall of Vietnam*. Farmington, Mich.: Lucent Books, 2002.

Levy, Debbie. *The Vietnam War*. Minneapolis: Lerner Publications, 2004.

Steele, Philip. *Ho Chi Minh*. Chicago: Heinemann Library, 2003.

Uschan, Michael. *The Fall of Saigon: The End of the Vietnam War*. Chicago: Heinemann Library, 2001.

Warren, Andrea. *Escape from Saigon: How a Vietnam War Orphan Became an American Boy*. New York: Farrar, Straus & Giroux, 2003.

Willoughby, Douglas. *20th Century Perspectives: The Vietnam War*. Chicago: Heinemann Library, 2001.

Search tips

There are billions of pages on the Internet so it can be difficult to find exactly what you are looking for. These search skills will help you find useful websites more quickly:

- Use simple keywords instead of whole sentences.
- Use two to six keywords in a search, putting the most important words first.
- Be precise—only use names of people, places, or things.
- If you want to find words that go together, put quote marks around them.

Places to visit

**National Museum of
American History**
On the National Mall
at 14th Street and Constitution Avenue, N.W.
Washington, D.C.
tel.: (202) 633-1000

**National Museum of the
United States Air Force**
1100 Spaatz Street
Wright-Patterson AFB, OH 45433
tel.: (937) 255-3286

**National Vietnam Veterans
Art Museum**
1801 South Indiana Ave.
Chicago, IL 60610
tel.: (312) 326-0270

Vietnam Veterans' Memorial
900 Ohio Drive, S.W.
Washington, D.C. 20024
tel.: (202) 426-6841

Where to search

Search engine

A search engine looks through the entire web and lists all sites that match the words in the search box. It can give thousands of links, but the best matches are at the top of the list, on the first page. Try **google.com**

Search directory

A search directory is like a library of websites that has been sorted by a person instead of a computer. You can search by keyword or subject and browse through the different sites like you look through books on a library shelf. A good example is **yahooligans.com**

GLOSSARY

addict person who cannot stop
doing something or using something

ally countries that is on the same side as
another country during a war

ambush surprise attack

ammunition bullets that are fired from
a weapon

artillery large mounted guns that fire
shells or missiles

assassinated murdered

battalion large military unit made up of
300 to 1,000 troops

booby trap bomb or weapon that is set
off when a person touches an object
that appears to be harmless

campaign series of related missions that
form a phase of a war

cease-fire end to fighting

civilian person who is not in the
armed forces

climate weather conditions for a
certain area

Cold War rivalry between the Soviet
Union and the United States that
began after World War II and lasted
until the 1990s

colony country or area that is ruled by
another more powerful country

combat fighting

Communist person who supports
Communism, which is a system of
government where all the wealth is
shared equally

covert secret

demonstration group protest

deserted left without permission

destroyer fast, lightly armored
but heavily armed warship

detonated exploded

draft order someone into
military service

draft card official letter ordering a
person to enter the military

embassy government building of
one country that is located in a
foreign country

enlightens teaches

evacuate move to safety

grenade weapon that is filled with
explosives and can be thrown or
launched at a target

guerrilla soldier who is not part of a
regular army

gunship helicopter that is armed with
several guns or rockets

heroin harmful, illegal drug

horrified shocked

hostile unfriendly

hurricane severe storm with heavy winds
and rain

massacre killing of a large number of
innocent people

Medal of Honor top medal awarded by
the U.S. Army

MiG jet fighter made by the Soviet
Union and flown by North Vietnamese
pilots during the war

missing in action (MIA) term used to describe a soldier who does not return from a war alive and whose body is never found

monsoon season period of wind and rain in southern Asia

morale confidence or self-esteem

mortar small, portable cannon

napalm sticky gel made from gasoline that bursts into flames when it hits the air

outraged made very angry

patrol search for enemy troops

platoon small army unit usually made up of 16 to 44 men

prisoner of war soldier who is captured and put in prison by the enemy during the war

protest display of disapproval. A person who protests is called a protester.

racist someone who hates someone else because of the color of their skin

ration small amount of food given to people so they can survive

rebel person who fights against the people who are in power

refugee person forced to leave home, usually during a war

resolution formal decision that is agreed upon by a vote

rice paddy area where rice is grown

sniper hidden soldier who shoots enemy soldiers from long distances with a special gun

Soviet Union country that once spread across northern Asia into Eastern Europe and included what is now Russia. Also known as the U.S.S.R.

Special Forces top soldiers in the U.S. Army

spider hole small one-person hole that is covered with leaves

supply line means of getting food, medicine, and ammunition

surface-to-air missile (SAM) missile launched from the ground to destroy enemy aircraft

surgery medical operation

tear gas type of gas that makes your eyes fill with tears

torpedo missile that is fired underwater

torture beatings and pain inflicted on prisoners, often to get secret information out of them

tour of duty period of time spent in active military service

tripwire wire stretched close to the ground that sets off an explosion when touched

truce agreement to stop fighting

veteran person who served in the armed forces